D0982097

Prayer Training
and Strategy for Kids

Stephen Kendrick and Alex Kendrick
with Amy Parker

illustrated by Lisa Manuzak

Nashville, Tennessee

Stephen Kendrick is a speaker, screenwriter, and producer whose film credits include *Facing the Giants, Fireproof, Courageous,* and *War Room.* Stephen coauthored the *New York Times* best sellers *The Love Dare* and *The Resolution for Men.* He also serves on the board of the Fatherhood CoMission. Stephen and his wife, Jill, have six children.

Alex Kendrick is a screenwriter, actor, and movie director whose film credits include *Facing the Giants, Fireproof, Courageous,* and *War Room.* Alex is a featured conference speaker and coauthored the *New York Times* best sellers *The Love Dare* and *The Resolution for Men.* Alex and his wife, Christina, also have six children.

Amy Parker has written more than twenty books for children, teens, and adults including the best sellers *A Night Night Prayer, My Christmas List, Frederick,* and two Christian Retailing's Best award winners. Amy and her husband have two children.

Published by B&H Publishing Group, Nashville, Tennessee
BHPublishingGroup.com

978-1-4336-8869-0
Dewey Decimal Classification: C248.32
Subject Heading: PRAYER / GOD / SPIRITUAL LIFE

1 2 3 4 5 6 • 19 18 17 16 15

Introduction: The Power of Prayer

To my prayer warriors:

Did you know that God created you to have a relationship with Him? He *wants* you to talk with Him. And one of the main ways we talk to God is through prayer. It's a powerful gift God has given each of us.

In this big world, we sometimes can feel powerless against the problems we face, both in our personal lives and throughout the world. But prayer can be a shield, a tool, a spiritual weapon we can use to connect directly to the Creator of the universe and to combat the evil around us. This book will show you how to raise up that shield, use that tool, and sharpen that weapon.

Prayer is a gift that has no doubt changed the course of history. From heroes in the Bible to our country's leaders and our very own lives, prayer has shaped us and sheltered us. In the book of Psalms, King David left us a record of his desperate, personal prayers to Almighty God. His son Solomon put in a simple request for wisdom, and God made Solomon the wisest man in the world. And God's own Son, Jesus, modeled for us how to pray. The Pilgrims, when settling this country, clung to prayer as they battled harsh winters, hunger, and deadly disease. Since then, national prayer has been called for regularly by the leaders of our country—from the Continental Congress in 1775 to President Abraham Lincoln in 1863. President Harry S. Truman even signed a National Day of Prayer into public law in 1952.[1] Prayer has no doubt carried God's people through so many difficult times—and it will carry you too.

---

1. National Day of Prayer, http://nationaldayofprayer.org/faq/

Sometimes prayer creates a lot of questions. *What's the best way to pray? Does God really hear me? Why do my prayers matter?* This book will guide you to find Scripture-rooted answers to those and many other questions.

But we don't want you to only *learn* about prayer. We want you to put your prayers to work! So in the back of this book, you'll find a section of tear-out pages to create and journal your very own prayers. You don't have to wait until the end to use them. Flip through them—now, if you want—and start your adventure!

You'll also see this symbol (the logo from the film *War Room*) as a visual reminder of the process that creates a powerful prayer life. We'll explain more as we go, but keep an eye out for it. Plus, we've included a large diagram, with each part of the logo explained, for you to tear out and take with you (see pages 126–127).

Our goal is to give you a strategy to harness the incredible power of prayer, right now, right where you are. With that power on your side, your path will be clearer, your relationship with God will be stronger, and your future will be filled with the fingerprints of Almighty God.

We need you. We've already prayed for you and everyone who reads this book. And we can't wait to see how your prayers will change the world.

Keep asking, keep searching, keep knocking!

Your friends,
Stephen and Alex Kendrick

Contents

Introduction 3

Chapter 1: What Is Prayer? 7

Chapter 2: Why Should I Pray? 17

Chapter 3: What Should I Pray For? 25

Chapter 4: Does God Really Hear Me? 35

Chapter 5: Where Do I Pray? 43

Chapter 6: Why Do My Prayers Matter? 51

Chapter 7: What's the Best Way to Pray? 59

Chapter 8: Is There a Wrong Way to Pray? 69

Chapter 9: When Should I Pray? 77

Chapter 10: Will God Answer My Prayers? 85

Put Your Prayers to Work! 95

Chapter 1: What Is Prayer?

Effective prayer begins with Christ.

What Is Prayer?

A Relationship with God

"For God loved the world in this way: He gave His One and Only Son, so that everyone who believes in Him will not perish but have eternal life." —*John 3:16*

To understand prayer, you must first understand the overwhelming love that God has for you. Even though God is awesome, perfect, holy, and pure, He is also a very loving Father. Love is God's nature and who He is (1 John 4:8). He does not love us because we are always so lovable—we aren't. He loves us because He is so loving. He made you and absolutely adores you—even more than your parents ever could. Hard to believe, right?

God's capacity for love is something that we can't even comprehend. So however much you're imagining that God loves you right now, it's a billion times that. Times infinity.

Prayer is really just talking to *that* God—the Creator of the universe who has this deep, unimaginable love for you. Jesus tells us in John 15:7, "If you remain in Me and My words remain in you, ask whatever you want and it will be done for you." That verse—and our prayer lives—begin with a relationship with Jesus. If we seek Him, let Him guide us, and "remain" in Him by staying close to Him, our desires are going to change and start lining up with His desires. And then whatever we ask for will be things that He wants to give us.

As you learn more about prayer, you'll have lots of questions. But whenever you do, just go back to God's great love for you. Start there, with that love, and know that He is a perfect Father. He is listening.

As you start your journey through this book, talk to your heavenly Father. Ask Him to help you learn more about Him and draw close to Him as you read. Ask Him to show you how to pray and be an effective prayer warrior for His kingdom. And ask it all in Jesus' name. If you aren't sure about your relationship with God and wonder if you're going to heaven, see pages 99–100.

What Is Prayer?

A Conversation with God

Don't worry about anything, but in everything, through prayer and petition with thanksgiving, let your requests be made known to God.—*Philippians 4:6*

When you talk to your friends, what do you talk about? The goal you made in a soccer game? That you're mad at your brother? How you're hoping for a new dog?

You can talk about the same things with God. The verse above says you can talk to Him about everything—from your smallest wishes to your scariest fears. When something goes great, you should thank Him for that gift. And when there's something you really want, you can tell Him that too. If you get distracted when you pray, ask God to help you focus. He wants you to pour out your heart to Him.

You can be sure that God is listening, just as if you were talking to a friend. But unlike your earthly friends, God has the power to make all of your worries and fears work together for your good (Romans 8:28). He alone has the ability to give you the desires of your heart.

So when you're talking to your friends here on earth, remember that you have a powerful God in heaven who wants to talk to you too. Be sure to make time for Him. Then just wait and see how it changes your life.

What is something that makes you laugh? Tell it to God. What are you afraid of? Tell Him. Make a habit of talking to Him as often as you would talk to your friends. Lay out your Bible as a reminder, and whisper a prayer every time you see it.

An Understanding Friend

Therefore, since we have a great high priest who has passed through the heavens—Jesus the Son of God—let us hold fast to the confession. For we do not have a high priest who is unable to sympathize with our weaknesses, but One who has been tested in every way as we are, yet without sin.
—Hebrews 4:14–15

Jesus isn't just any friend. The book of Hebrews tells us that while He was here on earth, Jesus was "tested in every way." There is nothing that you're going through that He doesn't completely understand. And because He knows everything before it even happens, nothing you can tell Him will surprise Him.

Jesus understands your weaknesses. He has felt your hurts and concerns. He, too, has been beckoned by Satan and tempted to do ungodly things.

But this verse in Hebrews doesn't stop there. It says Jesus made it through the testing "without sin." Do you know what that means? He not only understands; He also knows how to overcome it—whatever *it* is that you're going through.

You can trust Him. He will understand. And He will help you through it all.

Tell Jesus everything—whatever you've done wrong, your worries, and your weaknesses. Pour it all out at His feet, and watch Him pick it up and make something beautiful from it (Isaiah 61:3).

What Is Prayer?

A Voice for Your Heart

In the same way the Spirit also joins to help in our weakness, because we do not know what to pray for as we should, but the Spirit Himself intercedes for us with unspoken groanings.
—Romans 8:26

We can talk to God whenever we want, and Jesus will always understand. But what about when we're so broken, so confused, that we can't even find the words to say what we're feeling. Can God still hear our prayers?

The answer is a humongous YES.

You may have already learned that there's only one God. This is true! But the Bible also describes God as being like a family of three persons who love each other and work perfectly together. God the Father, the Son, and the Holy Spirit are each called *God* in the Bible; but they are also described together as being one God. Because our minds are limited, we can't fully grasp

the awesomeness of God and how He is three in one, but He is! After Jesus died on the cross, rose again, and spent forty days with His disciples, His physical body ascended into heaven. But when Jesus went back to be with His Father in heaven, He sent God's Holy Spirit to help us. When you and I confess and turn away from our sins and trust God's Son Jesus as our Lord, then God the Father becomes *our* spiritual Father. We become His children, and God's Spirit then comes to be with us, wherever we are.

When we have a prayer that's just too difficult to put into words, the Spirit will help us, and God the Father will hear, know, and understand our needs—even when we can't fully express them with our words.

Take a minute to focus on your worries and needs and joys right now. Don't say them out loud this time but quietly in your heart ask God's Spirit to take over your thoughts, to take control of your problems and needs, and to help you honor Him with how you respond to each one.

What Is Prayer?

A Gift from God

"You did not choose Me, but I chose you. I appointed you that you should go out and produce fruit and that your fruit should remain, so that whatever you ask the Father in My name, He will give you."—*John 15:16*

For we are not presenting our petitions before You based on our righteous acts, but based on Your abundant compassion.
—*Daniel 9:18*

Because God loves us—He *chose* us—He has given us this gift of prayer. The King of all kings has invited you to His throne and wants to hear what *you* have to say.

Make the most of this priceless gift by sitting at Jesus' feet and seeking His guidance. In doing so, you unwrap the most wonderful gift the world has ever seen—a relationship with the Almighty God.

Who is someone famous or in history whom you would love to meet and talk to? Now think about the awesomeness of being able to speak to the Creator of the universe, the One who made that person. Take a moment to thank Him for the gift of prayer.

Chapter 2: Why Should I Pray?

Effective prayer begins with Christ.

Why Should I Pray?

God Cares About Your Life

Humble yourselves, therefore, under the mighty hand of God, so that He may exalt you at the proper time, casting all your care on Him, because He cares about you.—*1 Peter 5:6–7*

Why would you bother with this whole prayer thing? Why would God even care about your life? I mean, you're just an ordinary kid, right? Well, when the prophet Jeremiah tried that kind of crazy talk, God set him straight, really fast.

When God first called Jeremiah, He explained, "I chose you before I formed you in the womb; I set you apart before you were born. I appointed you a prophet to the nations" (Jeremiah 1:5).

God made it clear that He had created Jeremiah for a purpose. He had been planning this before Jeremiah was even born. So how do you think Jeremiah responded to the Almighty God?

"Oh no, Lord, God! Look, I don't know how to speak since I am only a youth" (Jeremiah 1:6).

It seems that Jeremiah, like many of us, needed a little reminder. So God gave it to him.

Do not say, "I am only a youth,"
for you will go to everyone I send you to
and speak whatever I tell you.
Do not be afraid of anyone,
for I will be with you to deliver you. (Jeremiah 1:7–8)

We sometimes forget that God is on our side. He has given us life, breath, and abilities. He wants our lives to be successful, to follow His plans. And we can only learn about those plans by spending time with Him.

Ask God to show you His plans for you and to help you understand and follow them. Then learn from Jeremiah and trust God's plans. Know that God will always prepare and strengthen you for whatever He calls you to do.

Why Should I Pray?

He Wants You to Know Him

"This is eternal life: that they may know You, the only true God, and the One You have sent—Jesus Christ."—*John 17:3*

The Bible tells us that true life, *eternal* life is knowing God and His Son, Jesus. But how is it possible to ever know someone as amazing as God? Job 36:26 admits that God is "beyond our knowledge." Still, James 4:8 promises, "Draw near to God, and He will draw near to you."

And it really is that simple.

"Draw near" every day, wherever you are. "Draw near" when you're scared or happy or sad. "Draw near" when you're confused about everything—even God Himself.

Run to Him like running for shelter during a thunderstorm. Tell God your secrets like you would tell your closest friend. In those moments, God will be right there, drawing near to you. And when you draw near to Him, He will bless you and show you a little bit more about how amazing and wonderful He is.

Take a moment, right now, to sit in God's presence. Ask to know Him better. Be still and know that He is God and is holding the universe together. Thank Him for giving you air right now to breathe and for keeping your heart beating.

Why Should I Pray?

He Wants You to Be Joyful

"Remain in My love. If you keep My commands you will remain in My love. . . . I have spoken these things to you so that My joy may be in you and your joy may be complete."
—*John 15:9–11*

What makes you happy? Ice cream with sprinkles? Sliding into home plate?

As the Creator of life, Jesus knows the secret to a joyful life. And He shared it with us: keeping His commands, remaining in His love. A relationship with Jesus is the only way to a truly joyful life.

Can sprinkles and sports bring us joy? Of course! But for complete joy in life, we must remain in the One who made it.

Ask Jesus for the strength to keep His commands. Focus on remaining in His love. And bask in the complete joy that it brings.

Why Should I Pray?

He Wants to Guide You

Trust in the Lord with all your heart, and do not rely on your own understanding; think about Him in all your ways, and He will guide you on the right paths.—*Proverbs 3:5–7*

The more you draw near to God, the better you will know Him. Daniel 11:32 says, "The people who know their God will be strong and take action." God will bless you with that strength and guide you in that action.

The proverb above was written by Solomon, the wisest man in the world. He warns us not to rely on our own knowledge and experience. He suggests that we trust God to guide our steps.

I don't know about you, but I'm nowhere near the wisest person in the world. I mess things up a lot, and I still have a lot to learn. So when the wisest person in the world suggests to me that I should trust God as my guide, you'd better believe that I'm going to listen.

You see, just as God created Jeremiah and knew him before he was born (see pages 18–19), He created us and knows us too. And who better to guide our lives and lead our paths than the One who created us?

God knows us even better than we know ourselves. He has a big plan for our lives. And He will guide us in those plans if we will just trust Him.

Be like the wisest person in the world today by allowing God to guide you. Turn your plans and your future over to Him and ask Him to direct your paths.

Why Should I Pray?

God Is Glorified Through Prayer

"Whatever you ask in My name, I will do it so that the Father may be glorified in the Son."—*John 14:13*

Through the process of prayer—
when you take your cares to God,
when you get to know Him,
when you are truly joyful,
and when you allow Him to guide you . . .
God is honored and glorified.

When this happens, some people will wonder what makes you shine. Some will wonder what keeps you hopeful. Some will ask about the source of your joy. And when they do, that's your chance to tell them (1 Peter 3:15).

Not everyone knows the true path to peace. Not every boy knows about a God who loves him. Not every girl knows that she can be held in His arms.

That's where you come in. You can be the one to share good news about God to the people you know and meet. That's when you can bring glory to God.

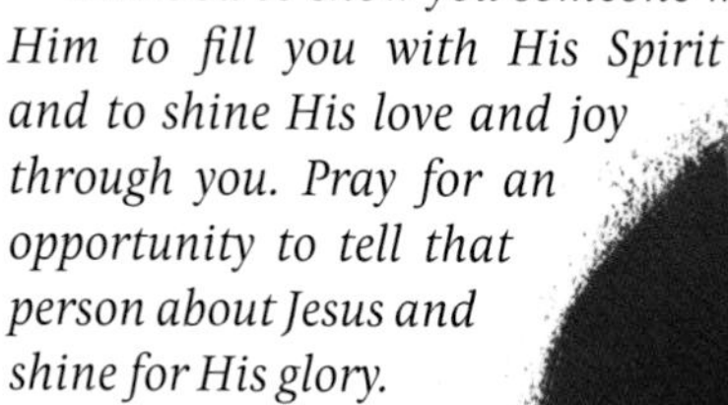

Ask God to show you someone who needs to hear about Him. Ask Him to fill you with His Spirit and to shine His love and joy through you. Pray for an opportunity to tell that person about Jesus and shine for His glory.

Chapter 3: What Do I Pray For?

Stay vertically aligned with God and His Word.

What Do I Pray For?

To Keep God's Word

Jesus answered, "If anyone loves Me, he will keep My word. My Father will love him, and We will come to him and make Our home with him."—*John 14:23*

A huge part of knowing God is knowing His Word. A huge part of serving God is doing what His Word teaches. And both begin with knowing what the Bible says.

The Bible is so much more than a big book of stories. It is God's love letter to His people, to you. It's a treasure map leading to the secrets to living life. It's a warning sign to help you avoid things that could harm you. It will teach you about God's character, how He wants you to treat others, and what He wants to do in and through you.

I know learning the Bible can seem like a lot—actually, *it is* a lot! But if you'll commit to reading a few minutes in the Bible each day, you'll be surprised at how much you will discover and grow.

You can start in Genesis or in the book of Matthew or anywhere at all! As you read a chapter at a time, you should ask God to speak to you. And when you finish reading through the Bible, you should flip back to Genesis and start all over again. You can learn something new every time! In the end, the rewards you reap are infinitely greater than the time you put in.

Just look at what Jesus promises in John 14:23: *to make His home with us.* When you think of all that will come from it, wouldn't you say that reading God's Word is a really important way to spend your time?

Ask God to guide you through His Word. Open it up each day, and spend a few minutes reading His personal letter to you. Ask Him to help you to know and love Him and to obey what He tells you to do.

What Do I Pray For?

That God's Will Is Done

Going a little farther, He fell facedown and prayed, "My Father! If it is possible, let this cup pass from Me. Yet not as I will, but as You will." —*Matthew 26:39*

When Jesus spoke the words above, He was in the garden, having an intense moment with God, His Father. Jesus knew what was coming. He knew that in a day's time He would suffer unimaginable pain and die on a cross. Yet Jesus still prayed that His Father's will would be done—no matter what.

In Genesis 22, when God told Abraham to sacrifice his son, Isaac, Abraham simply obeyed. He took his son and wood for a burnt offering and went exactly where God told him to go. Abraham wanted to obey God—no matter what.

Do you know the rest of Jesus' story? And Abraham's? Yes, Jesus still died on that cross—and as a result, everyone—the entire world—was offered forgiveness, God's saving grace, and everlasting life. Yes, Abraham was willing to sacrifice his son. But when Abraham proved his willingness to obey, God saved Isaac from death and then made Abraham's descendants as "numerous as the stars" (Genesis 22:17).

God's will isn't something that only benefits one person for a moment. God's will is for the benefit of the whole world for all eternity. So when you pray that God's will be done, you are praying for something much bigger than yourself. You're praying that the One with infinite wisdom will do what is ultimately best for His people —even if it doesn't seem like the best thing for you right now.

Consider God's will for your life. And when you're ready, ask that His will be done—even if it means doing difficult things.

What Do I Pray For?

Wisdom

Now if any of you lacks wisdom, he should ask God, who gives to all generously and without criticizing, and it will be given to him.—*James 1:5*

After Solomon became king, God appeared to him and said, "Ask. What should I give you?" (1 Kings 3:5).

Now I don't know about you, but if God asked *me* that question, I could think of *a lot* of replies. But Solomon answered with only one: "Give Your servant an obedient heart to judge Your people and to discern between good and evil" (1 Kings 3:9). Solomon's request wasn't for himself; it was for the benefit of all God's people.

And God was pleased. He told Solomon, "I will give you a wise and understanding heart, so that there has never been anyone like you before and never will be again. In addition, I will give you what you did not ask for: both riches and honor, so that no man in

any kingdom will be your equal during your entire life" (1 Kings 3:12–13).

Wisdom helps people to understand something, see the bigger picture, know what's more important, and then make the best decisions. Even if we're not kings, we still need wisdom every day. We may not be sitting on a throne, but our actions affect God's people and reflect God's kingdom.

All we need to do is ask. If we sincerely ask God for His wisdom, He will lead us and guide us as we make the daily decisions that affect eternity.

Think of all the things you would ask God for, then consider Solomon's request. Ask God to show you the importance of wisdom, and start praying for wisdom daily. God, "who gives to all generously," will give it to you.

What Do I Pray For?

Forgiveness

If we confess our sins, He is faithful and righteous to forgive us our sins and to cleanse us from all unrighteousness.—*1 John 1:9*

"And whenever you stand praying, if you have anything against anyone, forgive him, so that your Father in heaven will also forgive you your wrongdoing."—*Mark 11:25*

As much as we try to avoid it, as much as we try to be perfect, we all mess up. Romans 3:23 says, "All have sinned and fall short of the glory of God."

What really matters is how we deal with those mess-ups. And one big way is with prayer.

Jesus died on the cross to forgive us of our sins. We just have to ask. So when you go to God in prayer, be sure to confess anything that you've done wrong. He already knows everything, but He wants you to be honest with Him about it. Ask Him to forgive you. Ask Him to help you avoid that sin in the future. He tells us He will forgive.

It's also very important for us to forgive those who have sinned against us. Sometimes that can be harder than confessing our own sins. But the verse from Mark above makes it pretty clear that if we don't forgive others, then God won't forgive us.

This verse doesn't say that the person who wronged you has to ask for forgiveness. It doesn't say the person even has to know he hurt you. It says, "If you have anything against anyone, forgive him." We should go ahead and open up our hearts and forgive everyone, knowing that God is the perfect judge and will deal with each of them. We don't have to stay angry with anyone any longer.

Forgiveness matters. It matters to God, to your own happiness and health, and to the people around you. Make it a regular part of your conversations with God. Forgive often and quickly.

Has anyone hurt you? Have you hurt someone else? Talk to God now about forgiveness—both for yourself and for those who may have hurt you. Confess anything you have done wrong. And then fully forgive anyone who has hurt you.

What Do I Pray For?

Everything!

Pray at all times in the Spirit with every prayer and request.
—Ephesians 6:18

It's important to follow God's Word and His will, to pray for wisdom, and to grant and to ask for forgiveness. But equally important is maintaining your relationship with God through prayer.

Talk to Him all the time—about everything and anything at all. Talk to Him during the day. Talk to Him at night. And when you think you have nothing to say, just thank Him for being there.

In doing so, you will develop the habit of talking to Jesus. You will learn to listen to His voice. And most importantly, you will realize that He really is always there.

Talk to God right now. Tell Him about your day and whatever you're thinking, even if it's just that you're happy He's there.

Chapter 4: Does God Really Hear Me?

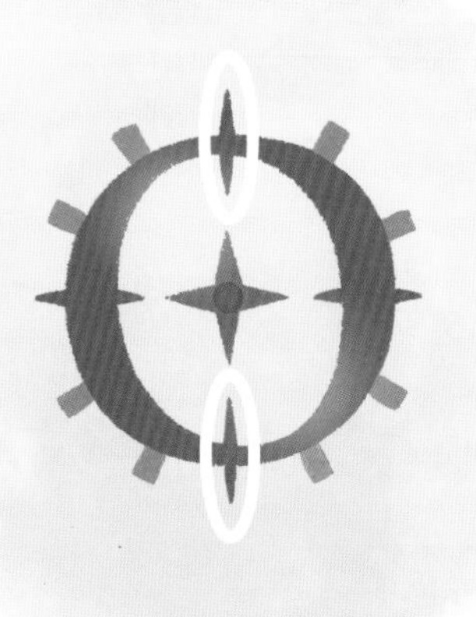

Stay vertically aligned with God and His Word.

He Hears the Hurting

I called to the LORD in my distress, and I cried to my God for help. From His temple He heard my voice, and my cry to Him reached His ears.—*Psalm 18:6*

Some of the most desperate pleas come from hurting hearts. And you'd better believe God hears those prayers.

They don't need to make sense. They don't even need to be spoken in words (see pages 14–15). They just need to be sent up to God.

So when you're disappointed, sad, in pain, or in need, cry out to God. And as with the prayers written by the psalmist in the verse above, know that your cry will reach His ears.

Is something bothering you that you need to take to God right now? Tell Him all about it, and let Him comfort you.

He Hears the Righteous

The righteous cry out, and the LORD hears, and delivers them from all their troubles.— *Psalm 34:17*

Are you doing what is right according to God? The Bible reminds us several times that doing what is right can affect your prayer life (see James 5:16; 1 Peter 3:12; and Psalm 34:15, to name a few).

We know that He hears our cries for forgiveness when we do wrong. But there is a powerful impact on our prayers when we speak from a place of "righteousness," or living the way God tells us to.

Your parents are more likely to respond to your requests when you're obeying them, not when you're breaking all their rules. Right? God is the same way. We're not going to get things right all the time. We need Jesus' forgiveness and help to stay clean before God. But God knows our hearts. He sees if our thoughts, attitudes, and efforts are turned toward what's right, and He will remember those efforts as we pray.

Talk to God about "righteousness"—what it means and how you can work on it together.

He Hears the Humble

And My people who are called by My name humble themselves, pray and seek My face, and turn from their evil ways, then I will hear from heaven, forgive their sin, and heal their land.
—2 Chronicles 7:14

Being humble means to stop thinking about ourselves and to put others first. It can be tough, and it can mean letting someone else take the spotlight. But sometimes we have to remind ourselves that we are on this earth to put God first and to help others. When we do that, our efforts may not be recognized by everyone here on earth. But they are appreciated by the One who matters most.

Jesus' life was a strong example of humility. The King of all kings no doubt deserved a plush king-sized bed, crowds of regal worshippers, and mountains of welcome gifts. But He was born

in a tiny, humble town, laid in a manger, and worshipped by poor, dirty shepherds. Jesus was later beaten, treated as a criminal, and laid in a borrowed tomb. Yet we know the rest of the story, don't we? Mark 16:19 says, "The Lord Jesus was taken up into heaven and sat down at the right hand of God."

Being humble isn't always easy, and it isn't always fun. But it sure beats being prideful. Proverbs 16:18 says, "Pride comes before destruction, and an arrogant spirit before a fall." God hates pride, and we should too. Whenever you're needing to feel important, remember that if you are a Christian, then you're already a beloved child of the King. That is greater than any reward here on earth.

Ask God to help you always stay humble. See what His Word says about humility and pride. (See Philippians 2:3–11 and James 4:6–10 for starters.) And look to the life of Jesus as your guide.

He Hears the Seekers

You will seek Me and find Me when you search for Me with all your heart.—*Jeremiah 29:13*

Are you actively searching for God? And what exactly does that mean?

Well, for one, you're reading this book. That alone shows that you're seeking a closer relationship with God. Each time you read your Bible, you are taking another step in your search. Every time you pray to God and He answers, you are finding out more about Him.

Moses was a dedicated God-seeker. He climbed to the top of a mountain—and stayed there for forty days and forty nights—just to be alone with God and hear what He had to say (Exodus 24:12–18).

That's when God gave Moses the Ten Commandments, the ones that still help us to this day. And it was there, on that mountain, where God actually allowed Moses to see His glory. Just from being in God's presence, Moses' face glowed with the radiance of God (Exodus 33–34).

Let us be like Moses and seek God, no matter what mountains we have to climb (Jeremiah 29:12–13). People around us may not always understand our search. But when our faces shine with the love, joy, and peace of God, they will know that what we seek outshines any treasures of this world.

Spend a little time seeking God right now. You can talk to Him, ask Him to help you know Him better, or just sit quietly in the warmth of His presence.

He Hears the Faithful

Know that the LORD has set apart the faithful for Himself; the LORD will hear when I call to Him.—*Psalm 4:3*

The Bible defines faith as "being sure of the things we hope for and knowing that something is real even if we do not see it" (Hebrews 11:1 NCV). Based on that definition, would you say that you have faith?

It can be hard sometimes to be "sure of the things we hope for." How can we know something is real if we can't see it?

We can't see the wind or electricity, but we know that they're there when we see trees move or the lights come on. We can't see God, but we see the evidence of God when we look in His Word, at the world He made, the lives He changes, or the prayers He answers. And that faith grows stronger every time we believe His Word, every time we trust and obey Him.

Believe that what God says is true. Trust and obey what He's telling you to do. Watch what happens. Never be afraid to put all of your faith in the one true God—even though you cannot see Him.

Talk to God about your hopes, and ask Him to help you to build a really strong faith by trusting His Word and obeying Him more and more every day.

Chapter 5: Where Do I Pray?

Remain horizontally aligned with others.

Where Do I Pray?

Pray Inside

Then Solomon stood before the altar of the Lord in front of the entire congregation of Israel and spread out his hands toward heaven.—*1 Kings 8:22*

King Solomon's men had just put the finishing touches on a brand-new temple. The king called together his priests and his people to celebrate and worship in this house of the Lord. Solomon stood in front of the people, raised his hands toward heaven, and prayed.

Thousands of years later, we are still gathering to worship and pray in the house of the Lord. There has been and always will be great power in those gatherings.

Whenever, wherever you go to church, consider it an honor to take part in this legacy of praying with God's people. God shows up when we gather in His name and pray in unity together.

The next time you're gathered at church, look around and thank God for these people walking alongside you in your faith. When people pray out loud, listen to how they pray and try to learn from the prayers of others how to better relate and talk to God.

Pray Outside

Then Jesus came with them to a place called Gethsemane, and He told the disciples, "Sit here while I go over there and pray."—*Matthew 26:36*

Praying in a church, surrounded by God's people is a wonderful thing. But you don't have to be in a building to speak to God.

Jesus chose a quiet garden as the site of one of His most desperate prayers. There, under the stars, surrounded by His Father's creation, "He fell facedown and prayed" (Matthew 26:39).

There's something about the beauty of nature that makes us feel closer to our Creator. Don't be afraid to speak to God in that closeness.

The next time you're outside, find a quiet place and close your eyes. Feel the wind blow, listen to the birds, and whisper a prayer to the mighty God who made it all and holds it all together.

Where Do I Pray?

Pray with Others

"Again, I assure you: If two of you on earth agree about any matter that you pray for, it will be done for you by My Father in heaven. For where two or three are gathered together in My name, I am there among them."*—Matthew 18:19–20*

We have more fun and get more done when we work together. The same is true when we pray together.

Jesus often taught His disciples how Christians should treat each other. One of those lessons was about the importance of praying with others.

Jesus tells us that when two people truly agree in prayer, then what they ask for will be done. He said when we come together in His name, He is right there with us.

Instead of fighting or being angry with one another, God wants us to forgive and love each other and pray for things together.

And when we do, He will come alongside us and bless us with answers to our requests. Then we can celebrate and rejoice together as He answers.

God hates it when His children are not getting along but loves it when we join hearts and hands to approach Him in unity.

Either with a friend or your mom or dad, ask someone to pray with you. When others pray out loud, you can silently pray along with them and say "Yes" or "Amen" in your heart to God as you agree with what they are asking from God. Feel the peace of Jesus after you finish praying together in His name. Then expect Him to answer in His timing.

Where Do I Pray?

Pray Alone

But when you pray, go into your private room, shut your door, and pray to your Father who is in secret. And your Father who sees in secret will reward you.—*Matthew 6:6*

Do you have a private room where you can pray? It's a great idea to have a special place of your own where you can meet with God every day.

It doesn't have to be a whole room, just a quiet area where you can focus on Him without being interrupted. It could be in your closet, a corner of your room, a chair somewhere, or even out in your tree house. No matter where it is, carving out a little place to talk to God reminds you—and shows others—that prayer is an important part of your life.

Personalize your prayer space to make it your own. You can color and hang your favorite Scriptures about prayer. You can draw pictures or write notes about the people you're praying for. And you can keep a journal of your prayers and the dates when they're answered. (See the back of this book for a lot of activities like these.)

The efforts you put into your prayer space will help to make it a more useful tool in your prayer life. Bible verses hung where you can see them will remind you of what God says about prayer. The notes and drawings will help you to pray regularly for those people until God answers. And writing down requests and answers in a prayer journal will build your faith as you see God answer your personal prayers time and time again.

Think of a quiet place where you can spend time with God. Go to that place daily, meet God there, and ask Him to help you make it a place of powerful prayer.

Where Do I Pray?

Pray Everywhere!

Therefore, I want the men in every place to pray, lifting up holy hands without anger or argument.— *1 Timothy 2:8*

Moses climbed up a mountain. Solomon stood in the temple. Jesus fell facedown in a garden.

Whether you're at church or at home, alone or with friends, on the playground or in your prayer place: you can pray.

It makes no difference where you are because God is *omnipresent:* He's everywhere, all the time. He can meet you wherever you are, whenever you call. He will hear your faintest whispers for help and your loudest shouts of praise.

The power is not in the place. The power is in the prayer—and most important, the God who hears it.

Right now, wherever you are, thank God for His constant presence and for listening to your prayers.

Chapter 6:
Why Do My Prayers Matter?

Remain horizontally aligned with others.

Why Do My Prayers Matter?

They Bring Us Closer Together

Dear friends, let us love one another, because love is from God, and everyone who loves has been born of God and knows God. The one who does not love does not know God, because God is love.—*1 John 4:7–8*

And I pray this: that your love will keep on growing in knowledge and every kind of discernment.—*Philippians 1:9*

Prayer can no doubt be a powerful tool for you as a person. But it also has a huge effect on God's people as a whole.

God calls us to love one another, to care for His people. The verse above even says that God *is* love. As His followers, we can be active examples of His love by praying for one another.

When you pray for people, something special happens. A bond is formed. You begin to care more for them and want God's best for them. Sharing how you are praying for someone is another way to tell that person that you really do care for him.

Paul's prayer in Philippians 1:9, for the church of Philippi, was that its love continue to grow "in knowledge and discernment." He was praying that the Philippians learn to see the needs of others and to show love by meeting those needs. And in praying for the church, Paul was showing his love for all of them.

Quite simply, prayer brings us closer together. It encourages us and ties our hearts together. And together, we have the power to better meet the needs of others. Sometimes praying for someone could do more to help them than if you gave them a million dollars! There is no limit to what the power of God can do.

Most important, prayer helps us to love one another. And that's what being God's people is all about.

Who have you been praying for? Who can you pray for today? The next time someone is worried or scared or in need, show your love by praying for him.

Why Do My Prayers Matter?

They Help Spiritual Growth

For this reason also, since the day we heard this, we haven't stopped praying for you. We are asking that you may be filled with the knowledge of His will in all wisdom and spiritual understanding.—*Colossians 1:9*

Just as healthy foods help your body to grow stronger, prayer helps your spirit to grow stronger. You can't always measure your spiritual growth like you can your physical growth, but I'll bet you'll notice a difference in other ways.

You're now more than halfway through this book. Think back to when you started reading, back to those first few pages. Where were you then in your prayer life? How has your spirit grown since you started?

See? Even though you can't measure it on the outside, you're growing on the inside. And that's where it counts!

Pray now and ask God to help you to grow closer to Him and more like Jesus every day.

Why Do My Prayers Matter?
They Restore Health

Is anyone among you sick? He should call for the elders of the church, and they should pray over him after anointing him with olive oil in the name of the Lord. The prayer of faith will save the sick person, and the Lord will restore him to health.—*James 5:14–15*

When you or a loved one is sick, of course you should get plenty of rest and maybe go to the doctor and drink your fluids. But also remember the most powerful medicine of all: prayer. James reminded the early church of this power. He told the people that God would hear their prayers of faith and could restore a sick person to health. The same is still true today.

You have a direct line to Jesus, the Great Physician. He knows exactly what is wrong, and He knows the right thing to do. He can guide the doctors, or He can just touch the sick person Himself. If you know of someone sick, don't be afraid to ask Jesus for help. He may choose to heal because you chose to ask.

Do you know someone who needs healing? Make an appointment with the Great Physician, and ask Him to get involved in a powerful way.

They Heal Hearts

Therefore, confess your sins to one another and pray for one another, so that you may be healed.—*James 5:16*

The health of your "heart"—your feelings, your emotions—is more important than your physical health. And one thing that can certainly make a heart sick is sin.

Doing wrong against each other can cause bitterness and anger and sadness to build up and weigh down our hearts. The book of James reminds us to confess those sins and to pray for one another so that we can be healed.

When you hurt someone's feelings, you should do the hard thing and do it quickly. Pray for strength and then go to that person, tell him you're truly sorry, and ask for his forgiveness. Ask God to forgive you too. Ask Him to help heal the heart of the one you've hurt.

Jesus has an answer for when people hurt you too. Matthew 5:44 says, "But I tell you, love your enemies and pray for those who persecute you." Yep, you heard that right: love your enemies. Pray for the people who hurt you, just as you would for anyone else.

Our prayers can make a big difference in the health of our relationships with others. Being honest and open when we mess up makes our friendships stronger. It builds trust when people know that we care about their feelings. And it heals hearts when we confess and pray for forgiveness.

Have you hurt someone lately? Has someone hurt you? Pray for that person. Forgive her or pray for forgiveness. Ask God to restore your relationship and make it stronger than ever.

Why Do My Prayers Matter?

They Grow God's Kingdom

Finally, brothers, pray for us that the Lord's message may spread rapidly and be honored, just as it was with you.
—2 Thessalonians 3:1

As a child of God, *you* can make a difference in His Kingdom. Each time someone chooses to follow Jesus, the Kingdom of God grows even bigger.

It's up to us as Christians to tell and teach the world about Jesus (see Matthew 28:18–20). And the good message we send out into the world should make others want to follow Him. When you act kindly, do the right thing, or pull together with others in prayer, the rest of the world notices. And you teach others about Jesus before even saying a word.

We need to pray regularly that more and more people will come to know Jesus. And we need to ask God to show us who we should share with and for Him to give us the courage and the words. Sharing the message is one of our biggest jobs and greatest joys as followers of Christ.

Do you know some people who need to know more about Jesus? Ask God to show you who you should reach out to with God's love. Add them to your prayer list, and ask God to help you care for them and share His love.

Chapter 7: What's the Best Way to Pray?

Get your heart right.

Through Jesus

For there is one God and one mediator between God and humanity, Christ Jesus, Himself human, who gave Himself—a ransom for all, a testimony at the proper time.—*1 Timothy 2:5–6*

Have you ever wondered why people sometimes say, "In Jesus' name I pray," at the end of their prayers?

Jesus gave Himself as a sacrifice here on earth to bridge the gap between God and us. He dealt with our sin and opened up the prayer line. He is the one "mediator" or go-between that connects us to the Father. So when we pray, we are speaking through Jesus, straight to God.

Jesus told His disciples, "If you ask Me anything in My name, I will do it" (John 14:14).

And Hebrews 7:25 tells us, "He is always able to save those who come to God through Him, since He always lives to intercede for them."

Let that soak in for a minute. Jesus is always ready to speak to God on your behalf. The One who has been here since the beginning of the universe, who sits at the right hand of God in heaven, who has God's ear, has also got your back. He is talking to God about you. Maybe even right now.

So when you call on heaven in prayer, ask in the name of Jesus, the One who died for you, who best knows you, and who is always able to save you and help you.

Talk to Jesus right now and thank Him for His sacrifice. Thank Him for always being there ready to act on your behalf.

As Jesus Teaches

Jesus is the ultimate Teacher when it comes to prayer. He both shows us by example and also tells us directly:

> Therefore, you should pray like this:
>
> Our Father in heaven, Your name be honored as holy.
>
> Your kingdom come. Your will be done on earth as it is in heaven.
>
> Give us today our daily bread.
>
> And forgive us our debts, as we also have forgiven our debtors.
>
> And do not bring us into temptation, but deliver us from the evil one.
>
> For Yours is the kingdom and the power and the glory forever. Amen.
>
> (Matthew 6:9–13)

He begins with giving honor to His Father in heaven. Then that God's will be done before anything else. With "daily bread," we should request enough to get us through the day, with no "worry about tomorrow" (Matthew 6:34). The sinless Jesus also tells us to ask for forgiveness while reminding us to forgive others. We should pray to be protected from temptation. And finally, Jesus shows us how to praise His Father, giving Him all the glory.

If you ever feel like your prayers need a little help, take a look at the model prayer that Jesus gave to us. But notice: He didn't say that this is *what* to pray but *how* to pray. So you don't have to repeat it word for word, but you should use it as a guide for how to talk with God.

Take a moment and pray through the Lord's Prayer. Either read it from the book or say it in your own words. Give thanks to Jesus for this example of prayer. Ask Him to guide you every time you pray.

In Obedience

Dear friends, if our conscience doesn't condemn us, we have confidence before God and can receive whatever we ask from Him because we keep His commands and do what is pleasing in His sight.—*1 John 3:21–22*

Because the eyes of the Lord are on the righteous and His ears are open to their request. But the face of the Lord is against those who do what is evil.—*1 Peter 3:12*

Ever hear that little voice in your head telling you not to do something bad? Or even that you *should* do something good? That's the "conscience" John is talking about above. It's a God given guide that tries to keep us on track, helping us to be obedient to God's will.

It's always important to be obedient, for lots of reasons. Ephesians 6 recalls one of the Ten Commandments: "Obey your parents as you would the Lord, because this is right" (v. 1).

Then it reminds us that this commandment comes with a wonderful promise: "so that it may go well with you and that you may have a long life in the land" (v. 3). A good life and a long life! That's a pretty good reason to listen to Mom and Dad, huh? (Not to mention, in doing so, you are also obeying your Father in heaven.)

When you know you've messed up, you'll approach God timidly. But when you are obedient, you have "confidence before God." When you are trying to do right, "the eyes of the Lord" are on you.

Each time before you pray, check your heart and conscience. Is it clean and clear? Have you been obeying God? If not, sincerely ask for forgiveness and for guidance in doing what is right.

Try it now. Ask God to search your heart and show you if there is anything that is displeasing to Him that you need to confess and stop doing. Clear conscience? Check! Now pray to God with confidence.

With Bold Faith

Therefore let us approach the throne of grace with boldness, so that we may receive mercy and find grace to help us at the proper time.—*Hebrews 4:16*

"Therefore I tell you, all the things you pray and ask for—believe that you have received them, and you will have them."
—*Mark 11:24*

The Bible is full of people with crazy-bold faith. They trusted God for great big things.

Moses led countless people out of slavery in Egypt to start a new life (Exodus 13). Young David stepped up to take down a bully giant (1 Samuel 17). Daniel spent the night in a den full of hungry lions (Daniel 6).

To a sick woman and to a blind man, Jesus said, "Your faith has healed you" (Mark 5:34; 10:52). And He told His disciples that if they only had faith the size of a tiny mustard seed, they could tell a mountain to move and that mountain would obey (Matthew 17:20).

Imagine that for a moment. Think of a tall, snow-capped mountain. Now, imagine telling it to move and seeing it move across the horizon. All because of a mustard-seed faith.

Bold faith is a big part of our story as Christians. And it should be a big part of our prayer life too. What mountain in your life needs to be moved? What is something big or hard that is too difficult for you to handle without God's help? Would you say that your faith is the size of a mustard seed? Approach God with a bold faith, and watch big things happen.

Oh, the things we can do with just a little faith!

Talk to Jesus about the mountains in your life. Pray about the big problems your family or church is dealing with right now. Now remember that God can handle any problem. Then muster up your faith, and say to your mountain, "Move!"

As a Child of God

Look at how great a love the Father has given us that we should be called God's children.— *1 John 3:1*

If you then, who are evil, know how to give good gifts to your children, how much more will your Father in heaven give good things to those who ask Him!—*Matthew 7:11*

Think about your parents for a minute, how much they love you, what all they do for you. Consider the money they have spent on you and the hours they've worked to provide for you, driving to ball games and recitals and field trips. Think of the lunches they pack and the laundry they wash. The shoes they tie. The noses they wipe. The hugs they give.

That's barely skimming the surface of what an earthly parent does for a child. And parents are imperfect sinners. Now imagine how much more your perfect heavenly Father wants to do for you.

When you pray, approach Him that way—as a loving Father, willing and waiting for your call.

Thank God for what He has done for you. Every breath and heartbeat is a gift. Now don't be afraid to ask Him to meet your needs and to prepare you to fully receive every good thing that He has planned and stored up for you.

Chapter 8: Is There a Wrong Way to Pray?

Get your heart right.

With Sin

If I had known of any sin in my heart, the Lord would not have listened to me.—*Psalm 66:18 (NCV)*

When Jesus died on the cross, He provided the ultimate sacrifice for our sins. All we have to do is turn to Him and believe, and we will be forgiven (1 John 1:9).

The sacrifice is made. The price is paid. We have no excuse. All you have to do is receive what He did for you and place your life into His loving control. And Jesus will clean and change your heart and toss your sins "as far as the east is from the west" (Psalm 103:12).

Because it really is that simple, we should bring our requests before God with a forgiven heart. When Moses stood before God at the burning bush, God told Moses to take off his sandals because he was standing on holy ground (Exodus 3:5). In the same way, we should remember the holy nature of God and ask Him to take the sin from our hearts.

Sin separates us from God (Isaiah 59:2). And as the verse explains above, it makes our prayers less effective. We shouldn't expect God to listen to our prayers if we don't listen to Him, if we refuse His gift of grace. So before you submit your requests and concerns to the Holy One, make sure you are soaked in the grace of His forgiveness.

Take a moment now to check your heart. Are there dark spots of sin that need God's forgiveness? Just ask the Holy of Holies to cleanse you with His grace.

With Bitterness

"But if you don't forgive, neither will your Father in heaven forgive your wrongdoing." — *Mark 11:26*

Think about someone who has been unfair to you, hurt your feelings, or made you mad. It may be a friend, a parent, or a sibling. Are you still angry with him, or have you forgiven him? God commands us to always choose forgiveness. That's when true healing begins. It feels really good to forgive someone, like a weight falling off your shoulders.

Let's do it now. Think of someone who has wronged you. Then say, "Lord, I choose now to fully forgive him. I'm turning what he did over to You."

See how simple that was? How did it feel?

It doesn't mean you won't ever think about it. And it certainly doesn't mean you can't talk to that person about it if you need to. But forgiveness is also admitting that you have no control over another person's actions and you are turning his actions over to God.

We shouldn't make requests from a loving God with angry hearts. We can't ask God to forgive us if we won't do the same ourselves.

Bitterness is a heavy burden. Deal with it quickly in prayer.

Ask God to guide you in dealing with bitterness. Make a commitment that you will become a master at forgiveness and never allow anger to poison your heart. Look to Him as an example of true forgiveness.

Is There a Wrong Way to Pray?

Words Without Meaning

"When you pray, don't babble like the idolaters, since they imagine they'll be heard for their many words."—*Matthew 6:7*

God likes humble hearts, not prideful prayers. When you pray, God isn't impressed with tons of words. He listens to your heart.

It doesn't matter if you speak English or Russian or Zulu, whether you discuss antidisestablishmentarianism or school, or if you deliver an hour-long monologue or a two-second cry for help.

He knows your situation and looks into your heart.

So when you pray, Jesus says, "Don't babble." Long, fancy words mean little to God. And they add very little to what you're trying to say in prayer. You can be real and get to the point.

So close your eyes, feel the presence of God, and offer up the simple and sometimes awkward whisperings of your heart. Always be respectful, but always be sincere.

And God will hear it for what it truly is: a beautiful and honest prayer from His child.

Whisper to your Father right now. Whatever is on your heart, whatever simple words may come, send them up sincerely and freely to the One who understands and cares the most.

Lacking Faith

But let him ask in faith without doubting. For the doubter is like the surging sea, driven and tossed by the wind. That person should not expect to receive anything from the Lord.—*James 1:6–7*

Have you ever watched the live report of a hurricane on TV? The guy is being pelted by rain as he tries to speak into the microphone. You can barely hear what he's saying over the roar of the wind. Then the camera pans out over the ocean. You can see the wild waves crashing violently on the rocks, shattering into a fine mist.

As James describes it, those waves are the prayers of a doubter. There is no control, no stability. They are thrown back and forth wildly and scattered in the wind.

When you ask for God's help, are you expecting good things or doubting the whole time? Do you pray knowing that He hears and it will be done? Or are you thinking all along, *He probably doesn't care. Why would God ever help me?*

I hope you have learned a lot about prayer and why God is eager to hear from you. If you are alive and your heart is beating, then you should already know that you never have any reason to doubt His love or His power. He wants you to trust Him and pray boldly, believing in faith.

But if you can't yet, then don't worry. Spend some time thanking Him and remembering His faithfulness in the past. Go back and read His Word and remember His promises about prayer and faith and how He loves His children. Then take a step of faith and pray boldly, believing, so that your prayers are not shattered in doubt.

Remember God's promises. Feel His love. And dare to ask for what you need, without a doubt.

Any Way but Jesus

Jesus told him, "I am the way, the truth, and the life. No one comes to the Father except through Me."—*John 14:6*

There is really only one way to pray, and that is through Jesus.

If you forget everything else, remember that one thing: Jesus is the way—the only way—to God, to eternal truth, and to eternal life.

You can pray sitting or standing or lying down. In a church or by a riverbank. With a mob of people or by yourself. Shouting or whispering or silently in your heart without saying a word.

But if you know Jesus, then you can do it all through Jesus. We approach God through Jesus' righteousness, not our righteousness. We can pray because of what Jesus did, not what we did. We ask in His name, not our name. Any other way will disappear like smoke in the wind.

Send up a thank-you today to Jesus for providing you the perfect way. And remember to pray about everything confidently, by asking all things in His name.

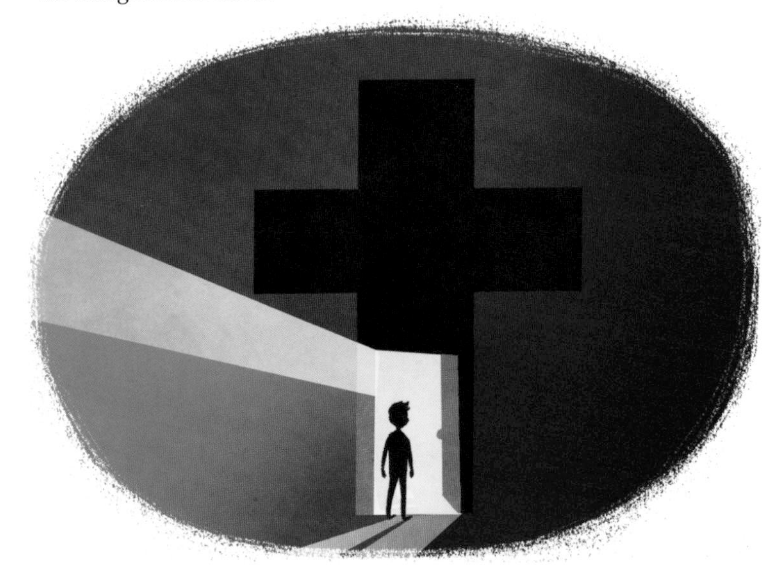

Chapter 9: When Should I Pray?

Pray specifically, strategically, and consistently.

When Should I Pray?

In Bad Times

Is anyone among you suffering? He should pray.
—James 5:13

Even people who hardly ever pray get this one right. They'll wait until they've tried everything. They've exhausted all other options. Then they call out to God as a last resort. It's as if their instincts kick in and tell them naturally who to call on for help.

And God does hear the desperate prayers of those going through the worst of times. He may even be allowing those times to happen to pull His children closer to Him.

No matter how close you are to God, bad times will still come. Neither Jesus nor His disciples had it easy, and your life likely won't be easy either. But that's why you talk to God regularly. You watch Him answer your prayers. You build your faith. Then when the bad times come, you'll already know: God's got this.

Knowing that will help you as well as those around you. James asks, "Is anyone among you suffering?" And if someone around you is, you already know how to help. Pray for him or her!

Point that person to the One who is always listening, the One who truly has the power to help. And when He answers in the bad times, it helps us all to draw that much closer to God.

Do you know someone going through a rough time? Pray for that person right now. Ask God to reveal His presence and power. And don't be shy about encouraging him or her to do the same.

When Should I Pray?

In Good Times

Is anyone cheerful? He should sing praises.—*James 5:13*

What do you say when someone gives you a gift? You know the answer (or else you'll get that look from Mom!). Your parents started training you to say thanks when you were little, asking, "Now, what do you say?" every time someone gave you a cookie or a card or a Christmas present.

Saying "thank you" doesn't always come naturally—especially when you're busy playing with your gift! But it is always very important to remember. Besides, gratitude isn't just for the benefit of the gift-giver. It also helps the receiver of the gift not to be as self-centered. It helps us all to remember that good things aren't always deserved, and they don't come every day.

The same goes when talking to God. He longs for us to develop very grateful hearts. Gratefulness adds joy to any situation. It silences complaints and helps jealousy and envy to melt away.

So what gifts has God given you? Salvation? Prayer? A caring family? A warm home? Awesome friends? His Word? Have you been so busy enjoying your gifts that you've forgotten to say thank you?

Remember to talk to God in the good times too. And to sincerely give thanks to Him for the wonderful gifts you've been given. Try it out.

Think of some of the wonderful gifts you've been given. Thank God for them today, and then add to the list tomorrow.

When Should I Pray?

In Urgency

The urgent request of a righteous person is very powerful in its effect.—*James 5:16*

Throughout his prayers, the psalmist says to God, "Hurry to help me!" five different times. We know that David wrote a lot of those psalms. And if David, a man after God's own heart (Acts 13:22), asked God to help him in a hurry, we can too.

The verse above says that an "urgent request" is "very powerful." And don't miss the use of that word *righteous* again. It means that you are right with God and sincerely trying to do the right thing. This was certainly true for David.

David spent a lot of time hiding and running from a jealous king. Again and again, God rescued David from being killed by King Saul. More than once, David was even allowed close enough to take the king's life. But David refused to harm God's chosen king. He honored God when it was hard and trusted God to still keep him safe (1 Samuel 24, 26).

David was right to trust the Lord. Not only did God keep David safe, He eventually made David king.

You should trust your urgent requests to God, too, knowing that He will hear your cries for help. Is there something that is weighing heavily on you right now? Are there any urgent needs or burdens in your family? Take a moment and pray about each one, and watch God put a fresh peace in your heart when you are done.

When Discouraged

[Jesus] then told them a parable on the need for them to pray always and not become discouraged.—*Luke 18:1*

Some days we're going to get down and discouraged. Sometimes we are going to lose hope and really feel like quitting.

Jesus knew this and told His disciples a parable about a persistent widow who refused to give up (Luke 18). Eventually, the "unjust judge" gave her what she wanted, just because of her persistence. Jesus pointed out that if a bad leader will help a widow who keeps asking, how much more so will a loving Father help His children when they keep praying for something.

No matter what our circumstances may be, our connection to God, through Jesus, is an endless source of hope. Psalm 31:24 reminds us, "Be strong and courageous, all you who put your hope in the LORD."

When you get discouraged or sad, let your tears be reminders to get alone and pray about your situation. Let prayer help you to become brave. To become strong again. And remember: your hope is in something much larger than the disappointments of this world.

Are you feeling discouraged? Talk to God about it. Ask Him to encourage you with His Holy Spirit. Then let your hope in Him bring light to the path ahead.

When Should I Pray? All the Time!

Pray constantly.—*1 Thessalonians 5:17*

Our goal is to be someone who doesn't *only* pray in bad times or urgent times or good times. Our goal is to be someone who prays anytime and *all* the time. Kids play constantly. Teens text constantly. Christians can *pray* constantly. It's when we call God in the morning and never hang up the phone all day long. Prayer should be an automatic response to every situation.

If we "pray constantly," we talk to God as naturally as talking to a best friend or a parent—and even *more* often. We tell Him the simple, small things and the serious, secret things. We talk to Him about everything, all the time. That may sound hard, but is it hard for you to talk all day when you are with your best friend?

When we are in constant conversation with God, we are not only telling Him about ourselves, but we are also learning His character. We are reminding ourselves that He is always there. We are receiving His encouragement and guidance in everything we do.

And that, my friends, is a pretty powerful prayer life.

Talk to God all day today. It doesn't always have to be out loud. It can be whispers in the moment or prayers in your heart. Imagine Jesus sitting there listening—because He is.

Chapter 10: Will God Answer My Prayers?

Pray specifically, strategically, and consistently.

Specific Prayers Get Specific Answers

Elijah was a man with a nature like ours; yet he prayed earnestly that it would not rain, and for three years and six months it did not rain on the land. Then he prayed again, and the sky gave rain and the land produced its fruit.—*James 5:17–18*

Miraculous things happened when Elijah spoke to God (1 Kings 17–18). Like what? An evil king experienced drought in his kingdom. A starving widow was blessed with an abundance of food. The same widow's son was raised from the dead. And fire fell from heaven in a stunning display, proving the existence and power of the One true God.

Elijah was a prophet, yet James reminds us that Elijah was imperfect like you and me, "a man with a nature like ours." Still his prayers yielded extraordinary results.

Elijah's prayers were strategic and specific. He would line them up with God's Word and God's will. And when Elijah spoke, God responded as strategically and specifically as Elijah had asked.

There is so much to learn from the life of Elijah, but one lesson is certainly in the way he prayed. Take some time to read more about him in 1 Kings 17 and 18. Then think about how this regular guy was able to summon the power of an Almighty God at his humble request.

How strategic are your prayers? Do you ask God for specific things? Ask God to show you what you should ask for and how to align your prayers with His will and desires. Then get busy praying! And ask Him to put the power of your answered prayers to work for His kingdom.

In His Own Timing

And so, after waiting patiently, Abraham obtained the promise.
—Hebrews 6:15

God works in His own timing. He promised to make Abraham into a "great nation" (Genesis 12:2). "Count the stars," God had told him. "Your offspring will be that numerous" (15:5).

There was only one problem. Abraham was the age of a great-great-grandfather and still didn't have any children. His wife, Sarah, laughed at the idea of having a child in her old age (Genesis 18:12) and suggested that they take God's promise into their own hands. In the end, their "solution" only ended up creating a lot of conflict. (You can read the whole story in Genesis 15–16, 18, 21.)

But God patiently waited. He waited until it was much too late for Abraham and Sarah to have children on their own. He waited until it would have to be a miracle. Only then did God fulfill His promise and give Abraham and Sarah their son, Isaac. And from that son came descendants as numerous as the stars.

We cannot fully understand God's perspective of time. He is not bound by any clock. He was here before the beginning of the universe, and He will be here into eternity. Peter notes, "With the Lord one day is like a thousand years, and a thousand years like one day" (2 Peter 3:8).

However, for us, as James bluntly puts it, "You don't even know what tomorrow will bring—what your life will be! For you are like smoke that appears for a little while, then vanishes" (James 4:14). It would be silly to think that we can plan our lives better than God.

So it is with prayer. He knows when a prayer should be answered and when we should wait longer. We should never let yesterday's unanswered prayer stop us from continuing to pray today. It's never easy to wait, especially for big things that affect our entire lives. But God's timing is always perfect. And His promises and answers are *always* worth the wait.

Are you patiently waiting for God to do something? To answer a prayer or fulfill a promise? You can trust Him to work in perfect timing. Until then, keep praying and keep trusting.

Will God Answer My Prayers?

Seek Him Until He Does

It is time to seek the Lord until He comes and sends righteousness on you like the rain.— *Hosea 10:12*

Let us hold on to the confession of our hope without wavering, for He who promised is faithful.—*Hebrews 10:23*

Imagine you are in a blazing desert. The sun blasts you from above as dust encircles your feet. The flaky ground crumbles beneath every step. The wind burns your skin. Your lips are cracked, your tongue is dry, and you're well beyond thirsty. You've been walking for days. Or has it been weeks?

Every pool of water has vanished as soon as you've reached it. But then you feel it. A cool drop soothes the back of your neck and rolls down your back. Then another. Is it real? Before you can finish the thought, a downpour of quenching rain covers you, soaking

you through. Smiling, you open your mouth to the sky and let each drop quench your thirst, drinking in the rain you've been seeking for so long.

Oh, how refreshing it is when God provides! Doubting and disobedience will only make you thirsty and weak. Yet "hope without wavering" is as refreshing as the rain.

Hosea reminds us to "seek the LORD" as we await the answers to our prayers. Doing so will help us to remember the ultimate purpose for those prayers: to draw us closer to the One who answers them and remind us of His power. God may wait and watch how we respond to the delay. Will we trust or run to something else to satisfy us?

Whenever you walk through the desert, always carry this quenching hope: "He who promised is faithful." He is always good even when circumstances are not.

Thank God for His faithfulness to always meet your needs. He always has. He always will. Those who will wait on Him will see Him open up the wonderful provision of heaven in due time.

Will God Answer My Prayers?

Trust Him When He Doesn't

"For My thoughts are not your thoughts, and your ways are not My ways." This is the LORD's declaration.—*Isaiah 55:8*

"Peace I leave with you. My peace I give to you. I do not give to you as the world gives. Your heart must not be troubled or fearful."—*John 14:27*

God is always listening to you. And He always wants what's best for your life. But the truth is, God will not always answer your prayers the exact way you may want. And that's really okay.

We could never completely understand God's methods or His reasons for doing what He does. His thoughts are not our thoughts. Our ways are not His ways. And He does not give to us "as the world gives." These are biblical truths and promises we can believe in—even if it means we can't completely figure God out.

We are not always going to ask for things that make sense or that will be best for us. You may want to eat chocolate chip ice cream for

every meal, every day. But your parents love you too much to give in to that wish. They know that in the long run, cavity-free teeth and a healthy, well-nourished body will benefit your life more than the short yumminess of ice cream.

God looks at our lives in the same way. He can see the future of every decision. When He considers the wishes of His children, He's considering all of His children, across the entire world, for all eternity. And He is working for the good of every single one (Romans 8:28). That includes you.

When God doesn't answer right away, consider His timing. And when He doesn't seem to be answering at all, remember the wisdom of His loving ways. He often is giving us something better than what we requested and is providing what we really need rather than what we think we want at that time.

Can you think of a prayer that you're glad *God didn't answer? Thank Him that He does answer so many prayers but also chooses to do what is best for His children.*

Keep Asking, Keep Searching, Keep Knocking

"Keep asking, and it will be given to you. Keep searching, and you will find. Keep knocking, and the door will be opened to you. For everyone who asks receives, and the one who searches finds, and to the one who knocks, the door will be opened."—*Matthew 7:7–8*

While you may be at the end of this book, you're only at the beginning of your prayer life with Jesus. We encourage you to take everything you've learned and apply it to your everyday relationship with Him.

But please don't stop there. Dig deeper. Look harder. Search further. We have only touched on the power and the beauty of prayer.

Knowing God is a never-ending search, a bottomless well of refreshing truth and goodness and life. Don't ever stop drinking from that well. His Word will teach you new things every time you read it. You will find fulfillment in Him that you never knew was possible.

Keep asking. Keep searching. Keep knocking.

And just as Jesus promised, you *will* find what you are looking for . . . in Him.

Put Your Prayers to Work!

It's time to put your prayers to work!

We not only want you to learn about prayer, but we also want you to harness and witness the power of those prayers! So throughout this section, you'll practice what you've learned within the chapters of this book.

There are prompts for prayers, activities to customize your prayer space, and a prayer journal to record your prayers as you go. The pages are meant for you to tear out and use, so don't be shy: put these prayers to work!

And when you've filled all these pages, grab a notebook and fill even more.

Remember:
Keep asking,
keep searching,
keep knocking!

Prayer Journal

Date	Praying For	Date Answered

Prayer Journal

Date	Praying For	Date Answered

Praying for Salvation

Fill this page with the words of John 3:16. As you write, think about what those words mean for you and those around you.

Praying for Salvation

Are you going to heaven when you die? God created you to love and honor Him. But every time you lie, steal, are mean, or disobedient, you are sinning against God. The Bible says that everyone has sinned (Romans 3:23) and deserves the punishment of death and separation from God forever (Romans 6:23). But God is merciful and He lovingly sent His Son Jesus to take our punishment by dying for our sins. Jesus now offers you forgiveness from your sins and a home in heaven if you will turn away from your sins and place your trust in Him. This is the best decision you will ever make.

If you haven't already done this, then think about the gift offered to you in John 3:16. If you want to accept God's forgiveness and to begin a new life in Christ, pray the prayer below or say it in your own words.

Dear heavenly Father,

I admit that I have sinned against You and need Your forgiveness. I believe that You are God's Son and died and rose again. I choose now to turn away from my sins and place my trust in You. Please forgive me, make me clean, and give me a home in heaven when I die. Come into my life and change me. Take control, Jesus, and help me to live the rest of my life for You. Thank You for Your gift of mercy and grace.

In Jesus' name I pray, Amen.

If you've prayed that prayer for the first time and really meant it, just know that this is only the beginning of a wonderful future with God. You can grow in your relationship with Him by praying daily, reading your Bible, getting baptized, and staying involved in a good church. Tell your parents and a leader at your church about your decision to follow Jesus. Each day, continue to seek God's ways and to obey His commands for your life. Also, tell others about Jesus who don't yet follow Jesus. May you grow and become closer to God and more like Jesus every day!

The Lord's Prayer

Our Father in heaven,

Your name be honored as holy.

Your kingdom come. Your will be done

on earth as it is in heaven.

Give us today our daily bread.

And forgive us our debts,

as we also have forgiven our debtors.

And do not bring us into temptation,

but deliver us from the evil one.

For Yours is the kingdom and the power

and the glory forever. Amen.

—Matthew 6:9–13

My Lord's Prayer

Rewrite the Lord's Prayer from Matthew 6:9–13 in your own words. Use it as a guide when you pray.

Praying for My Family

Draw a picture of your family. Hang it in your prayer space to remind you to pray for them.

Praying for My Family

Write a specific prayer for your family. What does your family need? What are you thankful for?

Praying for Others

Draw a picture of someone you find hard to love, someone who bothers you, or someone who may be mean to you. Remember to pray for him or her too.

Pray for Your Enemies

Fill this page with the words of Matthew 5:44.

A Faraway Prayer

Write a letter to a friend or family member who lives far from you. Tell him that you are thinking about him and praying for him. Then tear this out and mail it to him!

A Prayer for My Future

When you've filled out this page, tear it out, fold it up, and put it somewhere safe. On the outside, fill in the blank with the date of one year from today. Next year, open it up and see how you have changed.

Name: ______________________________

Date: ______________________________

Height: ______________________________

Weight: ______________________________

Grade: ______________________________

What I Want to Be When I Grow Up: ______________________________

What I Am Praying For: ______________________________

____

____

____

____

____

____

____

Do Not Open Until:

____

A Prayer for the Sick

Write a prayer for someone who is sick. Add him or her to your prayer journal. Then, after completing the opposite side of the page, tear out this prayer and give it to him or her.

A Prayer for the Sick

Fill this page with the words of James 5:14–15.

God Is . . .

Fill this page with words that describe what you have learned about God. Add to it as you learn more about Him.

God's Word Says . . .

List the truths and promises that you have learned from God's Word.

God Speaks . . .

Keep track of the ways in which you have heard God speaking to you. Whether it be through circumstances, His Word, or the whispering of the Holy Spirit, write it down when you hear Him speaking to you. Be sure to date each entry too.

God Speaks . . . *(continued)*

Spiritual Growth

Write a note to someone who has helped you to grow spiritually. It could be a teacher or pastor or the person who gave you this book. Describe what you have learned about prayer, and thank him or her for guiding your spiritual growth.

Mustard-Seed Faith

Fill this page with the words of Matthew 17:20.

Mustard-Seed Prayers

What are your biggest, craziest, mountain-moving prayers? List them here. And when you pray for them, pray with a mustard-seed faith.

Bull's-Eye Prayers

Do you have a specific, strategic prayer? Write it here and hang it in your prayer space. When that prayer is answered, use the other side of the page to do the same.

Bull's-Eye Prayers

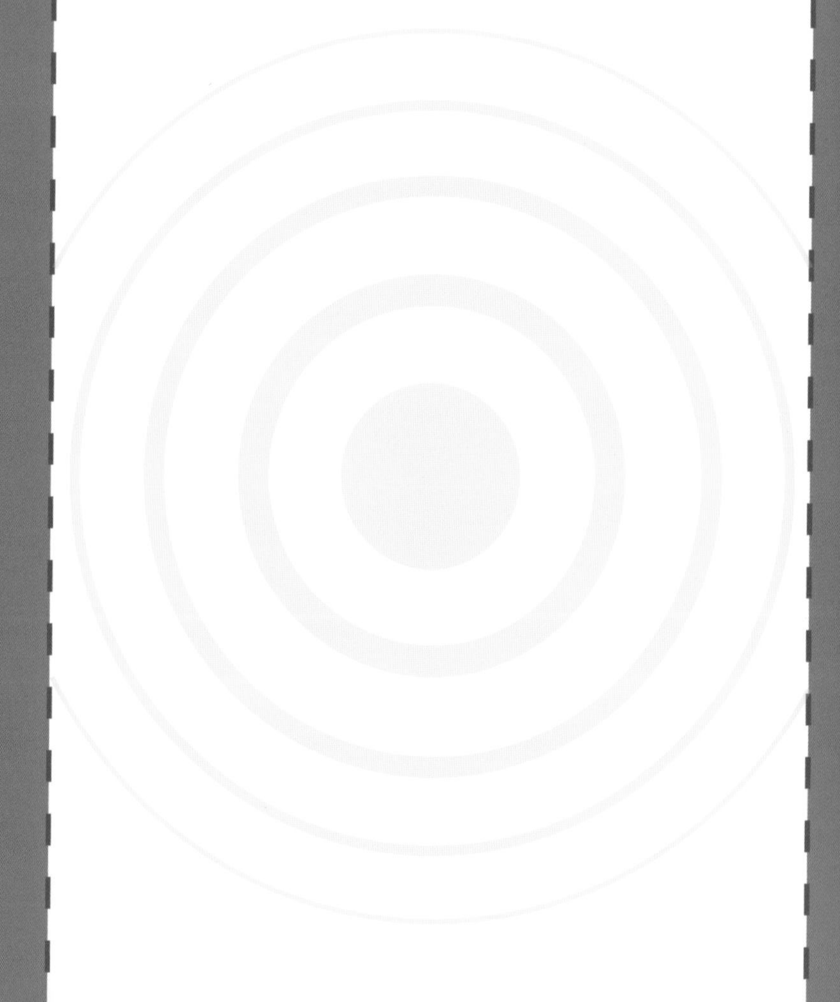

Thank You for . . .

Keep a running list of all the gifts God has given you. Remember to thank Him for these gifts.

1. ______
2. ______
3. ______
4. ______
5. ______
6. ______
7. ______
8. ______
9. ______
10. ______
11. ______
12. ______
13. ______
14. ______
15. ______

I'm Grateful for . . .

1. ______________________________

2. ______________________________

3. ______________________________

4. ______________________________

5. ______________________________

6. ______________________________

7. ______________________________

8. ______________________________

9. ______________________________

10. ______________________________

11. ______________________________

12. ______________________________

13. ______________________________

14. ______________________________

15. ______________________________

16. ______________________________

He Is Faithful

On this page, list all of the ways that God has shown His faithfulness.

The War Room Logo

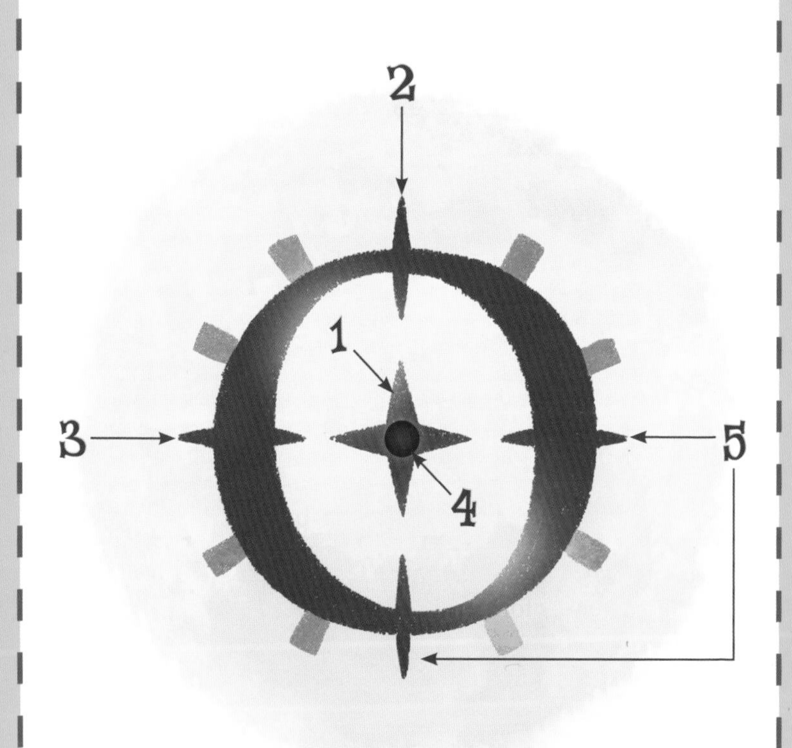

1. **Cross of Christ: Effective prayer begins with Christ.** As John 14:6 tells us, Jesus is the only way to God. Get to know Jesus and keep your relationship with Him strong. Your prayer life will be stronger because of it.

2. **Vertical line: Stay vertically aligned with God and His Word.** Learn about God and His will by studying His Word. His Word teaches us what He expects of us and how much He loves us. James 5:16 reminds us, "the urgent request of a righteous person is very powerful."
   A "right" life grows from knowing God and His Word.

3. **Horizontal line: Remain horizontally aligned with others.** Jesus teaches us in Mark 11:25 that our relationships with others can also affect the power of our prayers. Be sure that you are treating others the way you want God to treat you.

4. **Inner red circle: Get your heart right.** When you pray, come to Jesus with a heart free from bitterness and doubt, forgiven from all sin. Pray believing that you have received whatever you ask for (Mark 11:24).

5. **Crosshairs: Pray specifically, strategically, and consistently.** Be specific. Make every word count. And as Matthew 7:7–8 tells us, keep asking, keep searching, keep knocking.

May the power and glory of God be seen in your life as you draw closer and more in love with Him everyday, and may the joy of answered prayer be fresh on your lips as you shine like a star in this dark world that needs to see His light!

Parent Connection

Remember: Pray constantly.—1 Thessalonians 5:17

Read:
The best example of prayer in the Bible is probably in Matthew 6:9–13, when Jesus begins, "You should pray like this." He then goes on to show us—by example—how to honor God and His will, ask for what we need just for today, receive forgiveness and forgive others, call for God's protection from evil, and then turn all the glory back to God. We don't have to use Jesus' exact words when we pray, but these verses are a perfect guide for creating our own prayers.

Think:
1. How has your prayer life grown or changed by reading this book?
2. What is your favorite verse about prayer?
3. What prayers have you seen God answer?
4. If a friend needed help understanding prayer, where would you start? What would you tell him?
5. Who can you share the power of prayer with today?

Do: Create a prayer wall.
1. Find a quiet place in your house where you can sometimes be alone to pray.
2. Now get some paper. At the top, write down your favorite Scriptures about prayer.
3. Hang the paper on your prayer wall.
4. Each time you go to your prayer wall to pray, add reminders of what you're praying for. You can use the activities in this book or create your own.
5. Most important, go there regularly. Meet with God and let Him hear the whisperings of your heart.

Talk to God, get to know Him, and then watch the power of prayer at work in your own life.